Published by Arcadia Children's Books
A Division of Arcadia Publishing
Charleston, SC
www.arcadiapublishing.com

All images used © Shutterstock.com; p. 15 Hayk_Shalunts /
Shutterstock.com; p.24 Steve Cukrov / Shutterstock.com; p.30
Michael Gordon / Shutterstock.com; p.53 dshumny / Shutterstock.
com; p.67 James Kirkikis / Shutterstock.com; p.87 trekandshoot /
Shutterstock.com; p.88 bluejay23 / Shutterstock.com; p.89 AnjelikaGr
/ Shutterstock.com; p.94 pablopicasso / Shutterstock.com.

Cover illustration: Craig Yoe
Cover design: David Hastings
Page design: Jessica Nevins

Craig Yoe has written a TON of kids'
joke books! Yoe has been a creative
director for Nickelodeon, Disney, and
Jim Henson at the Muppets. Raised
in the Midwest, he has lived from
New York to California and has six kids!

CONTENTS

CITY JOKES

Where do you find the most haunted houses in LA?

Mali-**BOO**!

Did you hear the joke about Beverly Hills?

Yes, it is

HiLL AREAS

(hilarious)!

BEANY FACTOID:
Beverly Hills used to
be a lima bean farm!

Did you hear the joke about LA's tallest building, the Wilshire Grand Center?

No!

Never mind, it's over your head!

What starts with **L** and ends with **E** and has a million letters in it?

The Los Angeles Post Office!

Where do you go to listen to happy Mexican music in LA?

MERRY-achi Plaza!

Let's go to the
Laugh Factory.

Yes, its's a
HYSTERICAL landmark!

What do you give a dog at Venice Beach?

Mustard. It's the best thing for a **HOT DOG**!

What were the skater's last words?
"Hey, dude, watch this!"
How does a skater send her letters?
Airmail!

GUFFAWS AT GARVANZA SKATE PARK

What will your dad do if you win a big skateboard contest?

HEEL flip!

Where does your grandfather's wife like to go in LA?

To the **GRAMMY** Museum!

Looney LA Laws:

In LA, it's against the law to skateboard through a library or courthouse.

Which building in LA is the widest?

The Broad Museum!

Balloon Dog sculpture by Jeff Koons at the Broad Contemporary Art Museum

What building in Los Angeles has the most stories?

The Los Angeles Public Library!

Why do people like to work at the Capitol Records Building?

They go around in the best circles!

ROUND FACTOID: The Capitol Records Building was the world's first circular office tower!

.... --- .-.. .-.. -.-- .-- --- --- -..

Dot Dash Factoid:

The spire on the roof of the Capitol Records Building flashes the word "Hollywood" in Morse code.

.... --- .-.. .-.. -.-- .-- --- --- -..

Why is there a fence around the Angelus-Rosedale Cemetery?

People are **DYING** to get in!

What did the boat say when it pulled up to the Santa Monica Pier?

What's up, dock?

Where is the best place in LA to celebrate Christmas?

SANTA Monica!

Where's the best beach in LA for sunbathing?

Manhat-**TAN** Beach!

Manhattan Beach

Where's the best place to buy lumber in LA?

Brent-**WOOD**!

Brentwood

What's the best place for earning money in LA?

El Segun-**DOUGH**!

Where's the best place to inflate your tires in LA

Bel **AIR**!

Where does the math teacher like to go for vacation?

Los Angeles **COUNT**-y.

Los Angeles

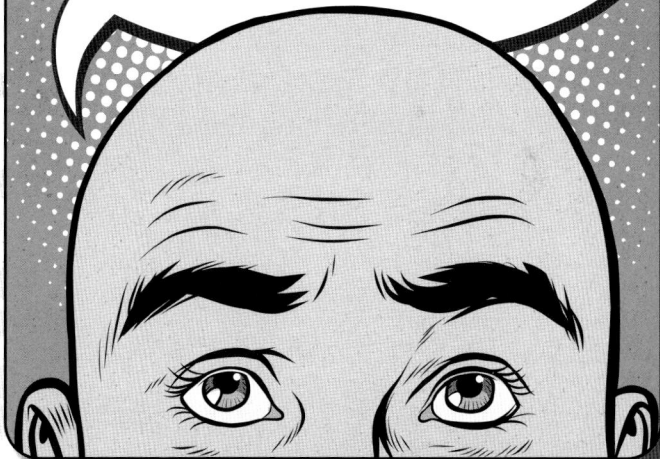

Where's the best place to get a toupee in Los Angeles?

BALDwin Park!

Santa Monica Pier

I just rode on the Ferris wheel at the Santa Monica Pier!

Wow, you really get around! LOL!

Metro Bike Share at Venice Beach

Why did the computer geek from LA take swimming lessons?

He wanted to surf the web!

What do you do if you don't have time to go to the City Walk?

Go to the City Run!

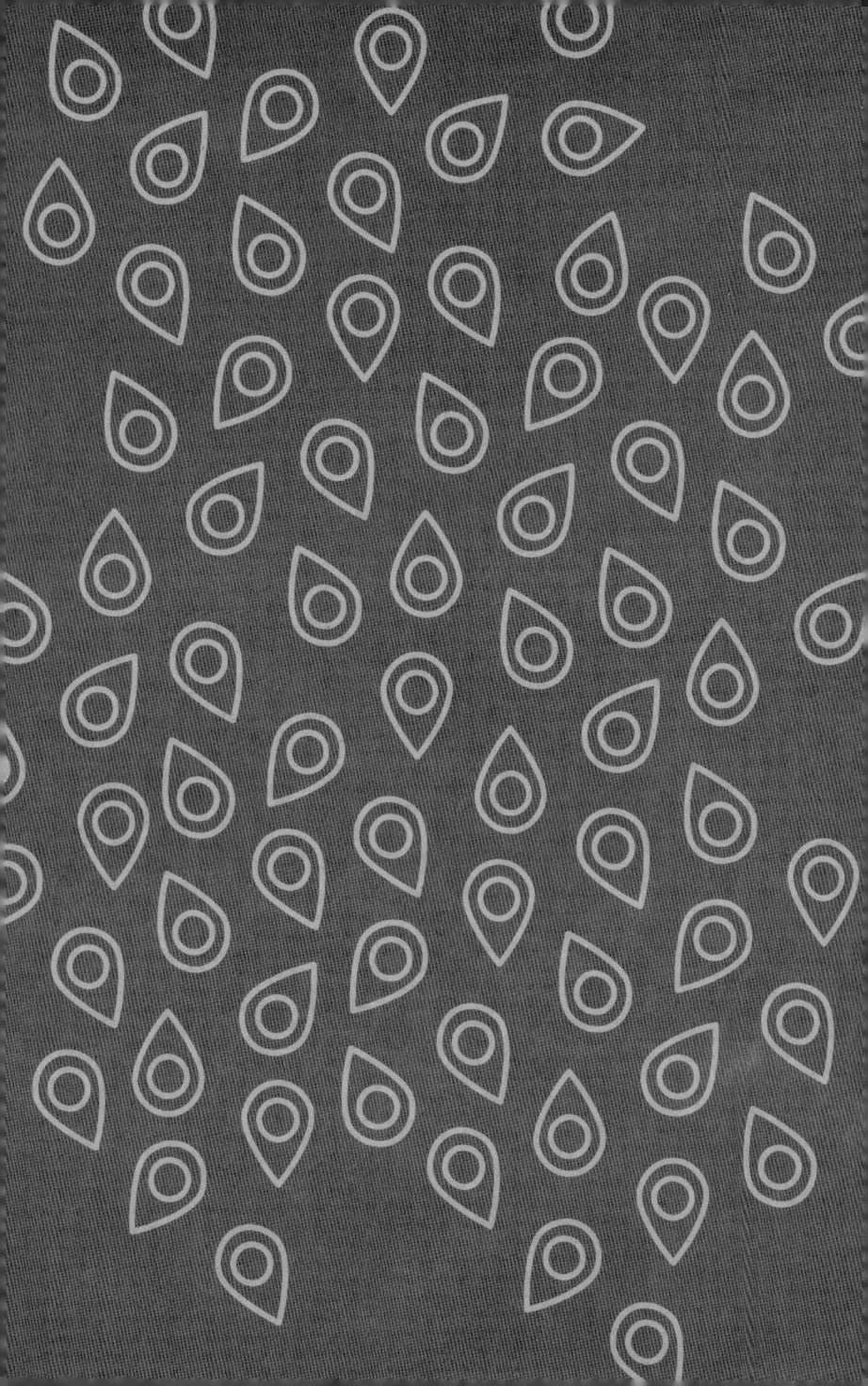

What do you say when your Mexican food from Olvera Street gets cold?

"**BRRRRR**-ito!"

FUN FACTOID

LA originally belonged to Mexico. It was annexed by the United States during the Mexican-American War in 1846.

Why did the police officer spread peanut butter on the 405?

To go with the traffic **JAM**!

**Pink's Hot Dog server:
I can tell you liked our hot dog!**

Tourist:

How's that?

**Server:
You ate it with relish!**

Did you see the hot dog stand in LA?

No, I saw it **SiTTiNG** in a bun!

Why did the hungry weightlifter go to Venice Beach?

To get some **MUSSELS**!

ORANGE YOU GLAD YOU HEARD THESE JOKES?

FUN FACTOID:

More orange trees grow in
Los Angeles backyards than in
orange groves!

KNOCK! KNOCK!

WHO'S THERE?

Orange!

ORANGE WHO?

Orange you glad I came for a visit?

Why did the orange go to the doctor?

He wasn't peeling good!

Why did the orange do well on his spelling test?

He was concentrated!

What does an aardvark like on its pizza?

ANTchovies!

Will my pizza be long?

No, it will be round!

Want to hear another pizza joke?
Oh, yes!
Aww, forget it– it's cheesy!

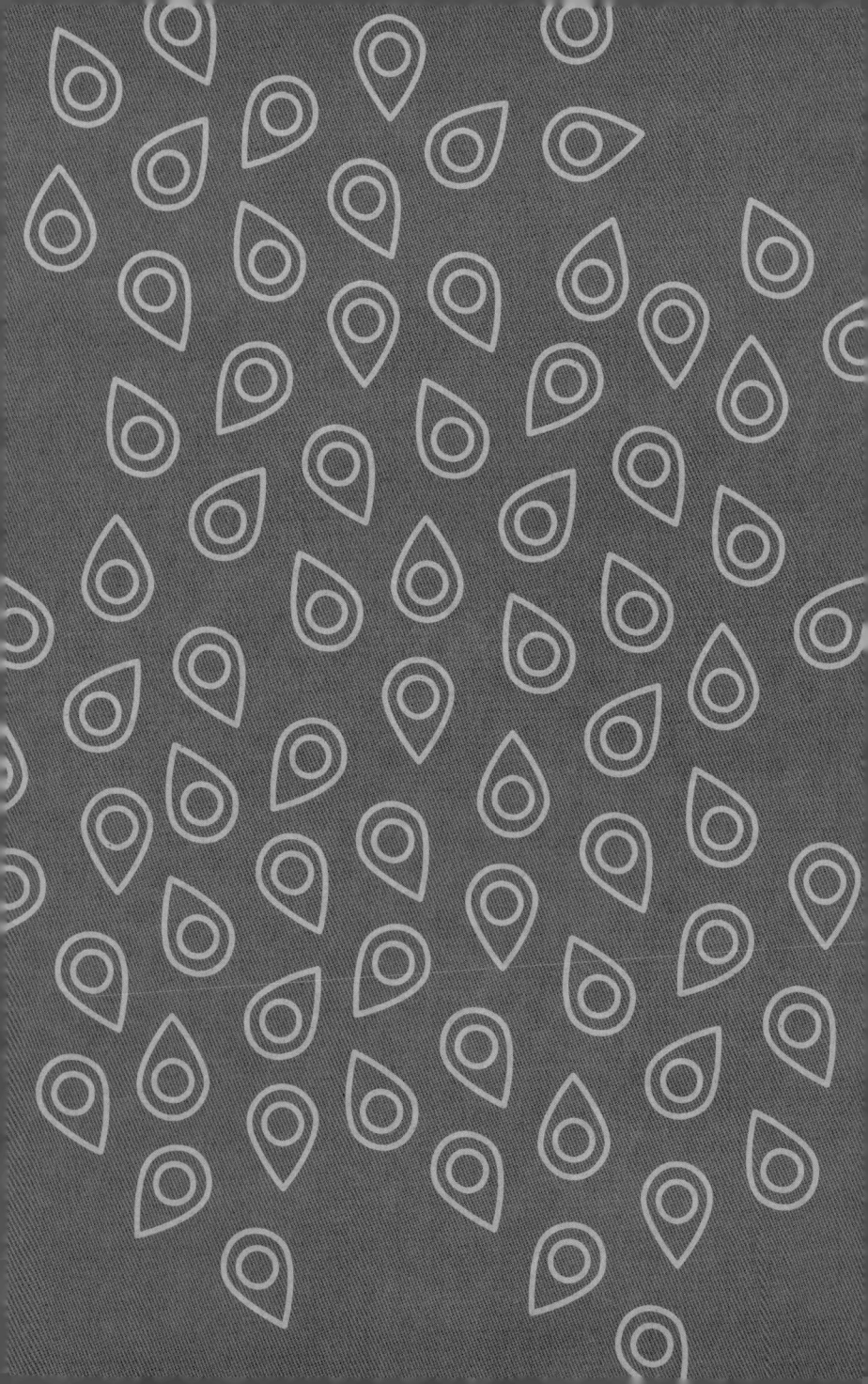

PUNNY BOOKS AT THE LOS ANGELES PUBLIC LIBRARY

LOS ANGELES WEATHER
BY SUNNY DAYE

RUSH HOUR: *LA STYLE*
BY DEE LAYS

BREAKFAST IN LA
BY HAMMAND EGGS

LUNCH IN LA
BY SAM WIDGE

WINDOW SHOPPING ON RODEO DRIVE
BY MANNY KIN

HOW I WON THE LOS ANGELES MARATHON
BY AARON QUICKLY

LA'S COMEDY CLUBS
BY VERA FUNNY

VENICE BEACH
BY SEYMORE BUNNS

HOLLYWOOD'S RICH AND FAMOUS
BY BILLY ANAIRE

CATCHING A WAVE
BY SIR FING

NOT JUST ROSES IN THE ROSE BOWL PARADE
BY FLO RIST

HOLLYWOOD ACTION STAR!
BY DARIN RESCUE

CELEBRITY HOMES
BY I.C. STARS

CALLING THE SHOTS
BY DEE RECTOR

WORKING AT FOREST LAWN
BY BARRY M. DEEP

LAID BACK IN SOCAL
BY JILL OUT

BIRD WATCHING AT BOLSA CHICA
BY C. GULL

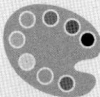

ART-Y PARTY

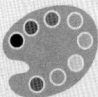

Jokes to tell at the Los Angeles County Museum of Art (LACMA)

Did you hear a wig was stolen from a movie star's Hollywood Hills home last night?

Yeah, the police are combing the area!

Why did the pirate love going to LACMA?

He loved **ARRRT**!

What do you get when you combine a snowman with Picasso?

Ice Cubism!

Tourist: Can we take pictures?

Guard: No, you have to leave them on the wall.

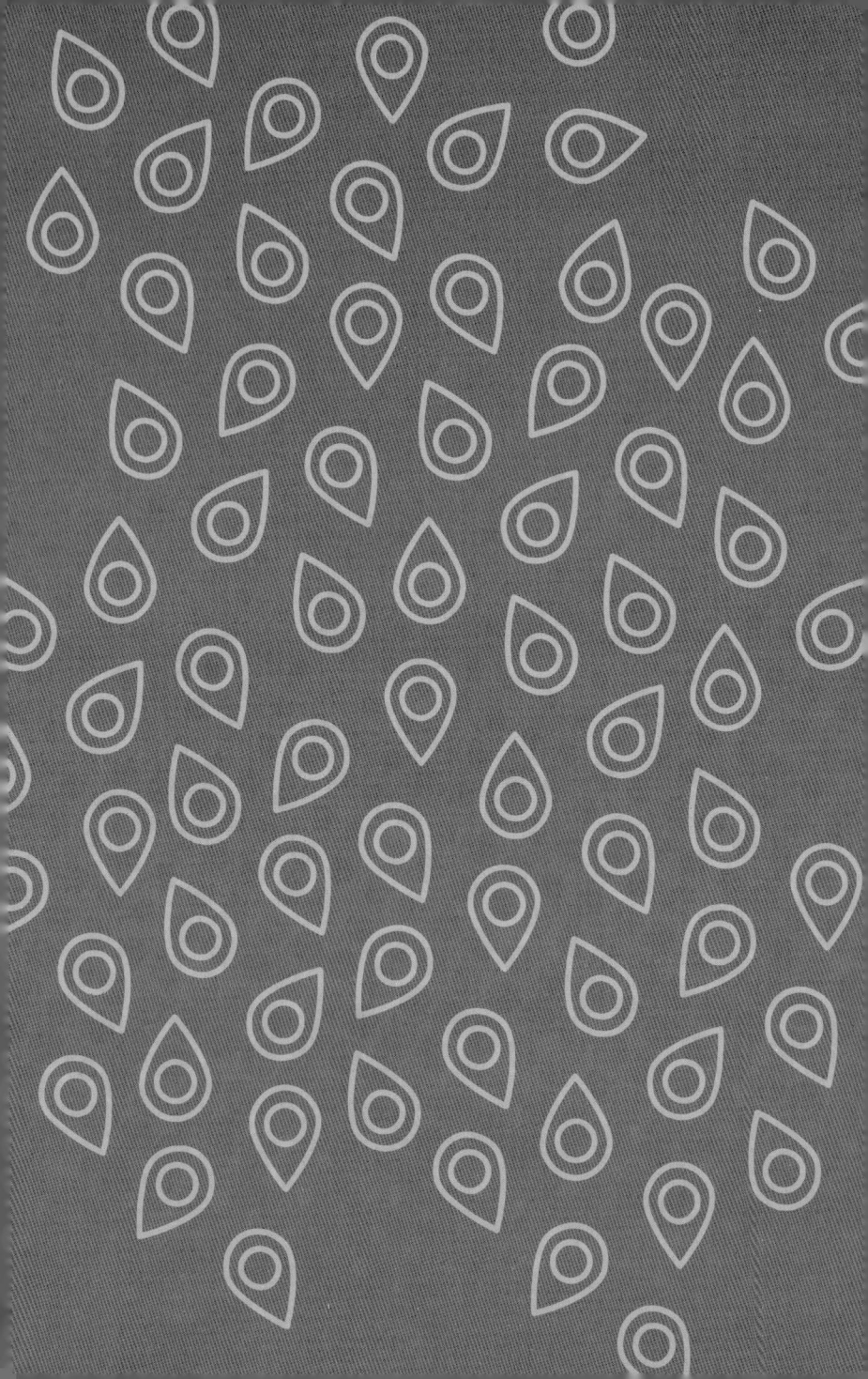

HIRE THIS GUIDE FOR THE GRIFFITH OBSERVATORY:

Hello! My name is:

 **Otto Dizwerld**

HIRE THIS GUIDE FOR THE VENICE FISHING PIER:

Hello! My name is:

 **Hy Water**

HIRE THIS GUIDE AT THE NATURAL HISTORY MUSEUM OF LOS ANGELES:

Hello! My name is:

 **Albert O. Saurus**

HIRE THIS GUIDE FOR THE GETTY MUSEUM:

Hello! My name is:

 **Getta Gide**

HIRE THIS GUIDE FOR THE HUNTINGTON LIBRARY:

Hello! My name is:

 **Anita Booke**

HIRE THIS GUIDE TO SHOW YOU THE LOS ANGELES ZOO:

Hello! My name is:

 **Ali Gator**

HIRE THIS GUIDE TO SHOW YOU WHERE TO FIND THE BEST PANCAKES IN LA:

Hello! My name is:

Dee Lish

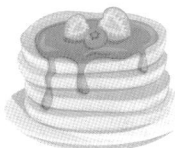

HIRE THIS GUIDE TO SHOW YOU LA'S COLLEGES:

Hello! My name is:

Ima Lerner

HIRE THIS GUIDE TO SHOW YOU THE LOS ANGELES PUBLIC LIBRARY:

Hello! My name is:

Lotta Shelffs

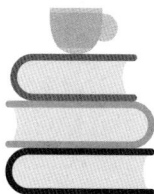

HIRE THIS GUIDE TO SHOW YOU LA'S COMEDY CLUBS:

Hello! My name is:

Shirley U. Jest

HIRE THIS GUIDE TO SHOW YOU THE MILDRED E. MATHIAS BOTANICAL GARDEN:

Hello! My name is:

Poppy Cox

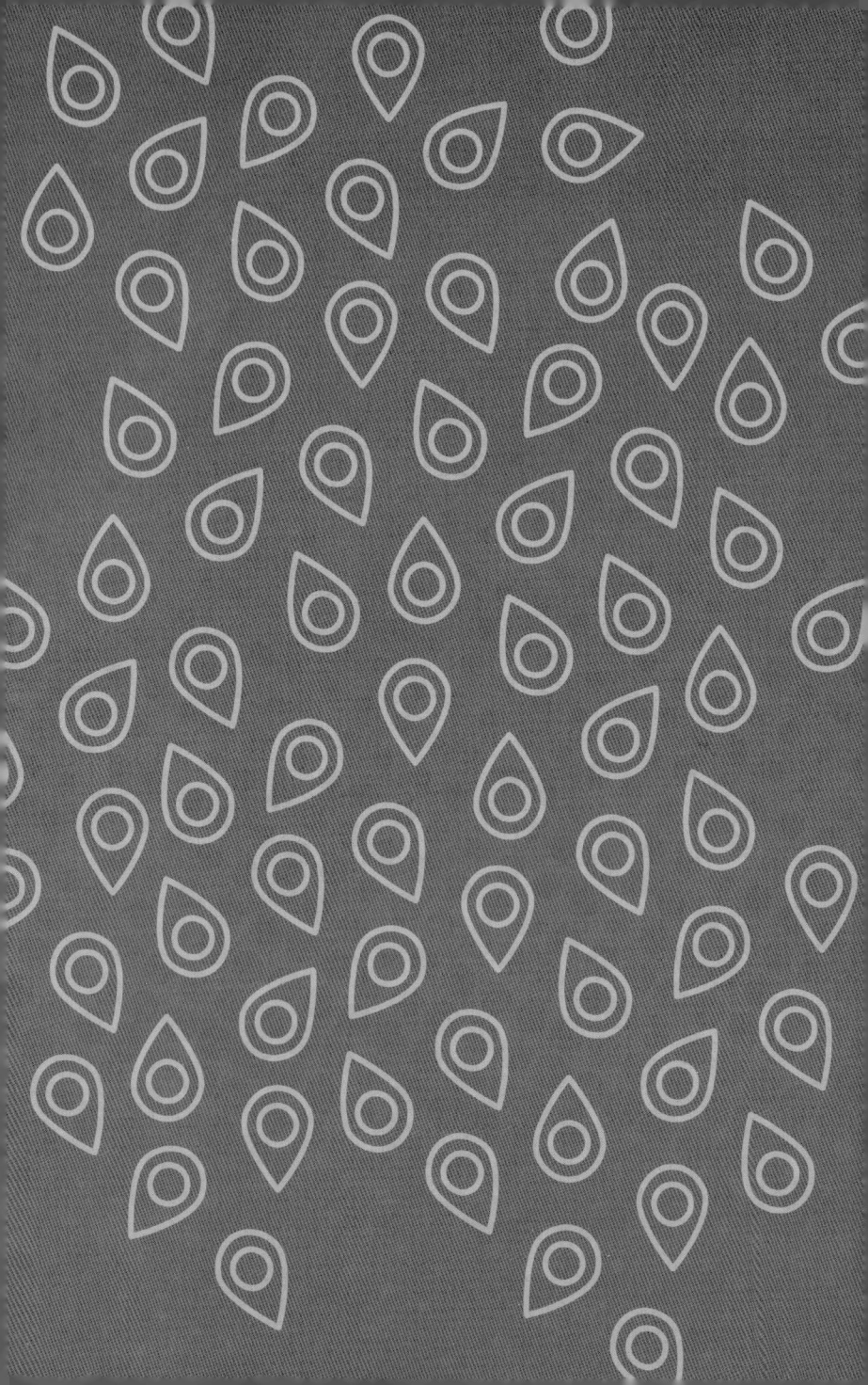

WHAT'S <u>ZOO</u> WITH YOU?

JOKES TO TELL AT THE LOS ANGELES ZOO!

What animal got called to the principal's office?

The cheetah!

Why is a giraffe such a good father?

Because he's someone you can look up to!

What has a jaguar's spots, an elephant's trunk, and a bighorn sheep's big horns?

The Los Angeles Zoo!

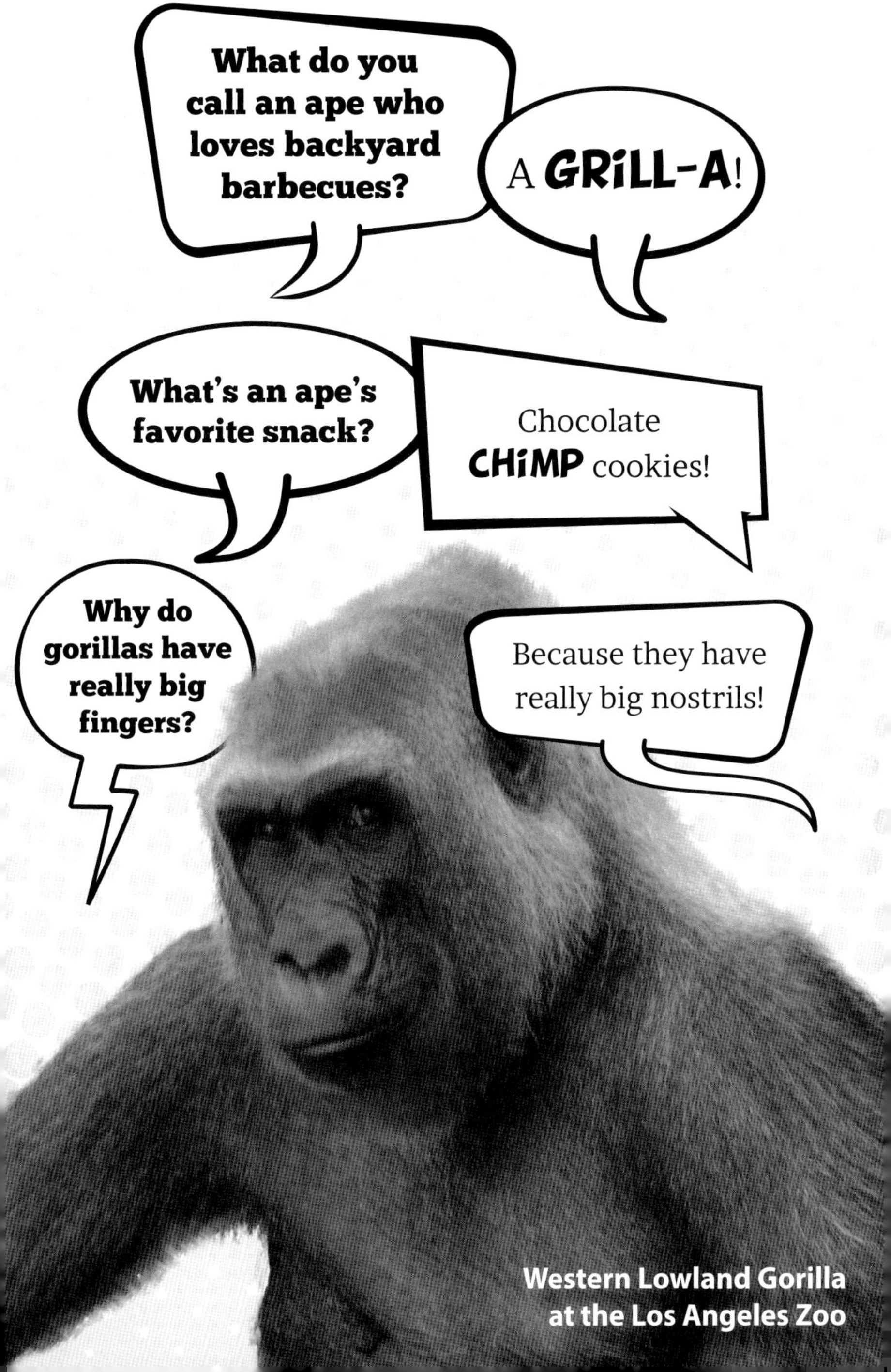

Western Lowland Gorilla at the Los Angeles Zoo

PINK FACTOID

The Los Angeles Zoo has one of the largest flocks of flamingos in any zoo in the world!

Fiona: How do you know when a flamingo is blushing?

Grace: You don't!

Flamingos at the Los Angeles Zoo

Charlotte:
How do you know when
a flamingo is mad?

Lia: She puts her
foot down!

James:
Do you want to
hear some more
flamingo jokes?

Violet:
Nope, I gotta flaming-GO!

Jake: Your dog was chasing a kid on a Metro Bike!

Declan: That can't be, my dog can't ride a bike!

Shhh! Don't tell!

Why was the tourist excited to see the dolphin at Santa Monica Beach?

It gave her life **PORPOISE**! LOL!

Why do whales like to swim in the saltwater at the Santa Monica beach?

Because pepper makes them sneeze!

What does an elephant wear to Santa Monica Beach?

Swimming trunks!

Why was the cow excited to visit Hollywood?

She loved going to the **MOOO**-vies!

HORSE LAUGHS AT SUNSET RANCH!

When does a horse talk?

WHiNN-EY wants to!

How long should a horse's legs be?

Long enough to reach the ground!

Which side of a horse has the most hair?

The outside!

Hilarity at the Heal the Bay Aquarium in Santa Monica

What happened when you called the Heal the Bay Aquarium?

They said my call would be recorded for training porpoises!

Why did the whale cross the road?

To get to the other tide!

What do fish take to stay healthy?

Vitamin Sea.

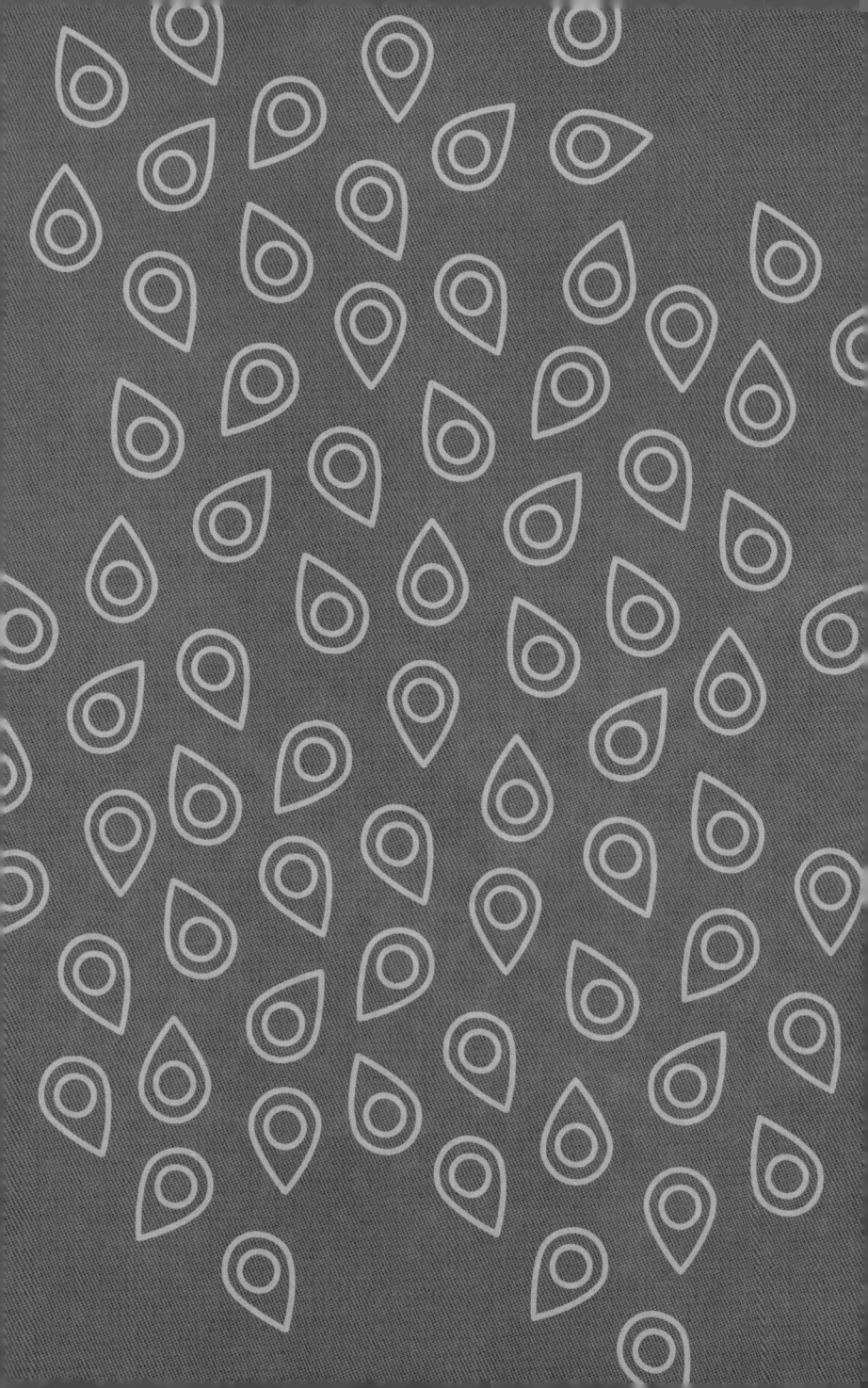

NATURE JOKES

QUAKING WITH LAUGHTER!

Shaky Factoid:
Southern California gets about 10,000 earthquakes every year.
(Most are too small to feel, though.)

What did one LA earthquake say to the other?
It's not my fault!

I don't think a big earthquake can happen.
You're on shaky ground!

What do you get when you combine a cow with an earthquake?

A MILKSHAKE!

What do you think of my earthquake jokes?

They're a groundbreaking experience!

No, really!

They crack me up!

So they made you laugh?

I was shaking uncontrollably!

What LA plant fits in your hand?

A palm tree!

FUN FACTOID:

The iconic Los Angeles palm tree is really a native of India and Southeast Africa.

What happens to a sunburned California orange?

It starts to peel!

Why does the mammoth at the La Brea Tar Pits have a trunk?

Because he would look silly with a suitcase!

Prehistoric Scene at La Brea Tar Pits

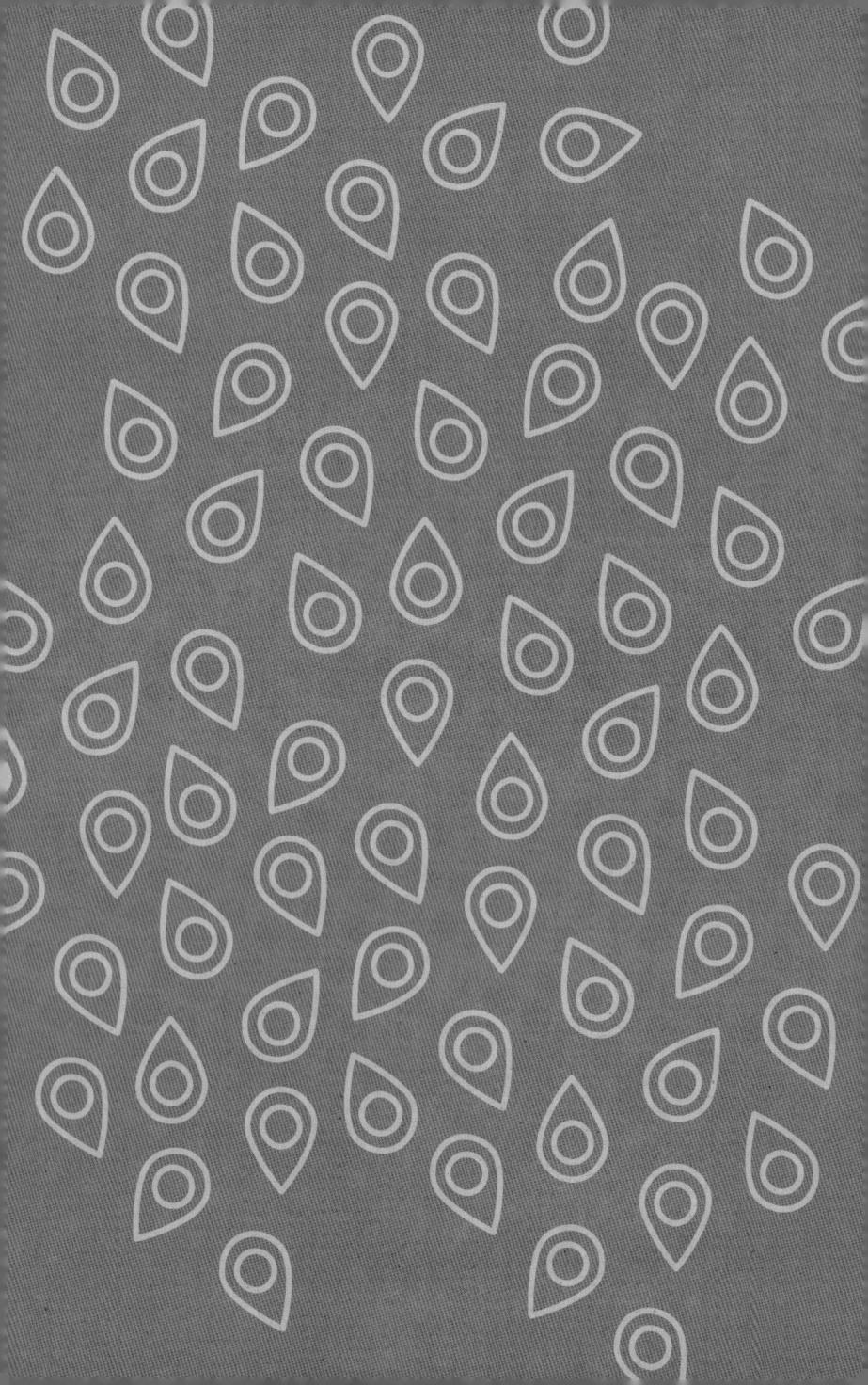

Which wave
won the race to the
Pacific Ocean shore?

Neither, they were
TiDE!

What does
a nose do at Santa
Monica Beach?

Go
BOOGiE
boarding!

Venice Beach

What did the sun bring to the party at Zuma Beach?

A light snack!

LA Wisecrack Wisdom:

Reading a book while tanning at the beach makes you, well, **RED**.

If you don't want to spend a day at Long Beach, where do you go for a quick dip in the ocean?

Short Beach!

HANG TEN HA-HAS

What kind of school do surfers go to?

Boarding school

How do surfers say hi?

They wave!

How do surfers take a bath?

THEY WASH UP ON THE SHORE!

What did the wave say to the surfer?

"Have a swell time!"

Why do you look so sad?

I'm surf *bored.*

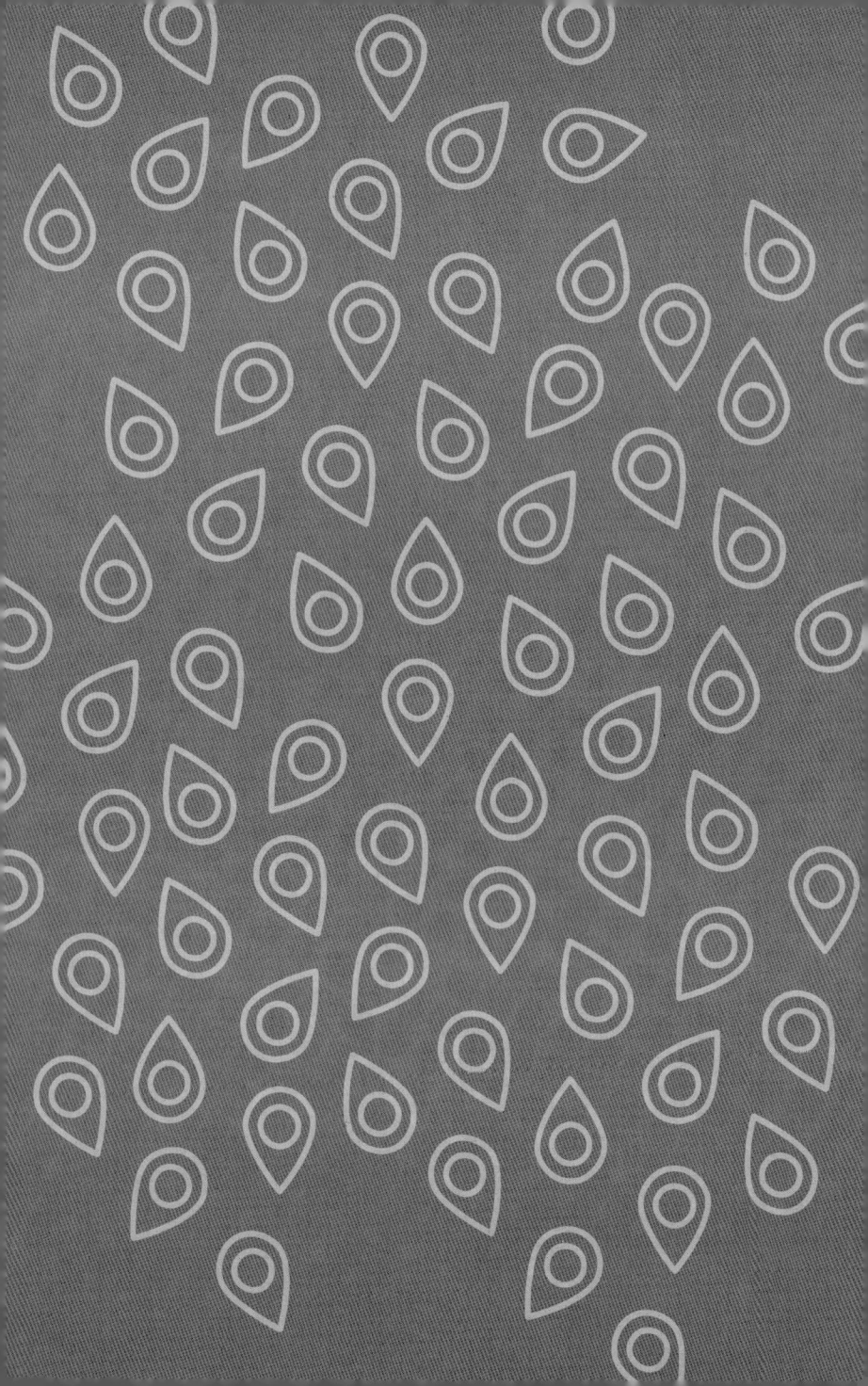

LA SPORT-Y JOKES!

What's a Dodger's least favorite *Star Wars* movie?

The Umpire Strikes Back!

Which basketball players have the best haircuts?

The Los Angeles Clippers!

Which team did the elephant try out for?

The LA Chargers!

What did the Angel's mitt say to the ball?

I'll catch you later!

Do you know what the enforcer on the Los Angeles Kings does?

Yes, of course!
Just checking!

What did the skeleton drive to the Anaheim Ducks game?

A Zam-bony!

Why did the defensive player for the LA Galaxy cross the road?

To get to the other slide!

eeek!

Which LA team members have the highest credit card bills?

The Los Angeles Chargers!

Which LA team likes to get down?

The Anaheim Ducks!

Which LA team is the best at fishing?

The Los Angeles Lakers!

Which LA team is on fire when they play?

The Los Angeles Sparks!

FUNNY THOUGHT

If a puck is flying through the air at a Los Angeles Duck, does he dodge? And if a ball is coming at a Los Angeles Dodger, does he duck?

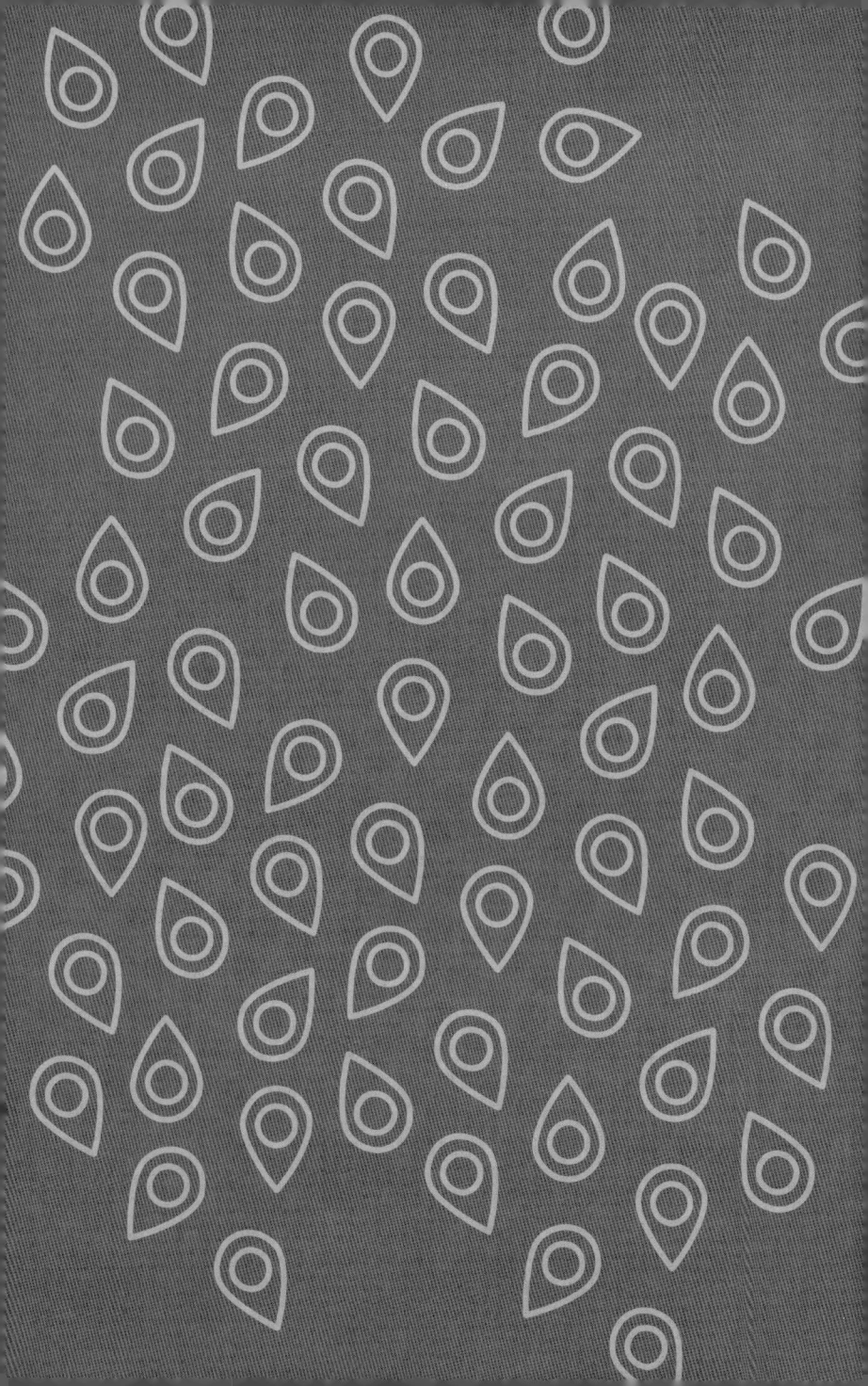

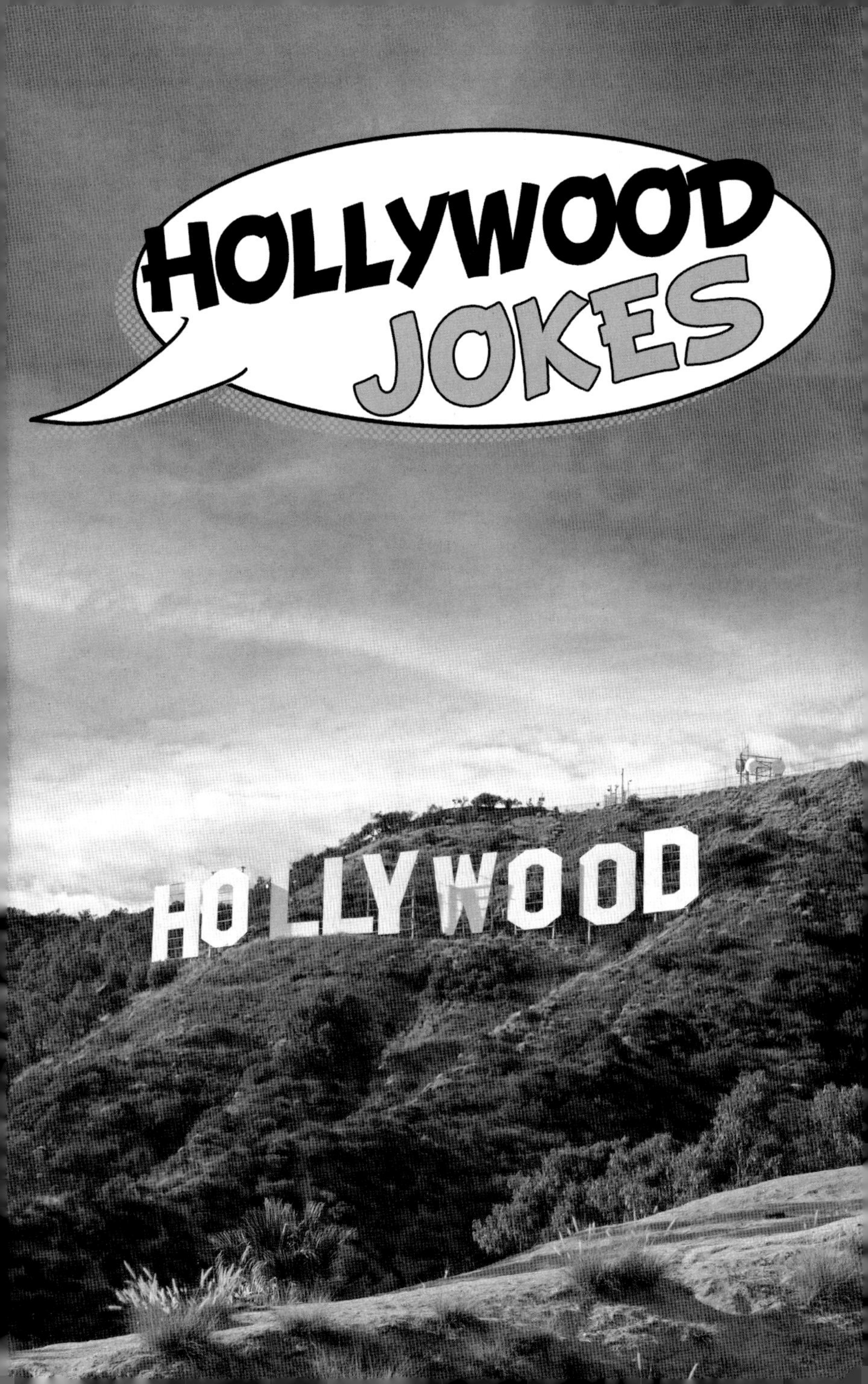
HOLLYWOOD JOKES
HOLLYWOOD

What do you get when you cross a dinosaur with a pig?

+ =

Jurassic **PORK**!

Which Transformer is the most positive?

OPTIMIST Prime!

How do you get to the Wizarding World of Harry Potter?

Go through the **DUMBLE**-door!

The Wizarding World of Harry Potter in Universal Studios

DISNEYLAND DIZZIES!

Why did Mickey Mouse go to outer space?

He was trying to find Pluto!

What's the best vehicle to drive to Disneyland?

A Minnie-van!

Why is Peter Pan always up in the air?

He Neverlands!

Pixar Pier at Disneyland

How does Mark Hamill feel at Venice Beach?

Luke warm.

How did he get there?

Ewok.

What kind of car does a Jedi master drive?
A *TO-YODA*!

Obi-Wan Wisdom: Don't eat your peas with a knife. Use the forks, Luke!

THE HOLLYWOOD WALK OF FAME FUNNIES

FUN FACTOID:
The Hollywood Walk of Fame has more than 2,500 stars, attracting over 10 million star-struck tourists every year!

TOM HANKS

Where can you find Picasso's star?

On the Walk of **FRAME**!

Where can you find a skateboarder's star?

On the Tony **HAWK** of Fame!

Where can you find the Human Torch's star?

On the Walk of **FLAME**!

Why are Hollywood stars so cool?

They have a lot of fans!

Why do people tell Hollywood actors to break a leg?

A movie needs a good cast!